Extreme
SNOW
SKIING

Virginia Loh-Hagan

45th Parallel Press

Published in the United States of America by Cherry Lake Publishing
Ann Arbor, Michigan
www.cherrylakepublishing.com

Content Adviser: Ned Rosenman, all-mountain and backcountry skiing, Jackson Hole, Wyoming
Reading Adviser: Marla Conn, ReadAbility, Inc.
Photo Credits: ©IM_photo/Shutterstock.com, cover, 1; ©VisualCommunications/istockphoto.com, 5; ©Christiannafzger/
Dreamstime.com, 6; ©bikeriderlondon/Shutterstock.com, 8; ©ZargonDesign/istockphoto.com, 11; ©PeteWill/istockphoto.com,
13; ©Michal Onderco/Shutterstock.com, 15; ©Alexander Ishchenko/Dreamstime.com, 17; ©Benjamin Haslam/Dreamstime.com,
19; ©Mountainpix/Shutterstock.com, 21; ©SMI/Newscom, 23; ©Photoimagesnz/istockphoto.com, 24; ©Aurora Photos/Alamy, 27;
©Jacomstephens/istockphoto.com, 29; ©Trusjom/Shutterstock.com, multiple interior pages; ©Kues/Shutterstock.com, multiple
interior pages

45th Parallel Press is an imprint of Cherry Lake Publishing.

Library of Congress Cataloging-in-Publication Data

Loh-Hagan, Virginia.
  Extreme snow skiing / Virginia Loh-Hagan.
    pages cm. -- (Nailed It!)
  Includes bibliographical references and index.
  ISBN 978-1-63470-017-7 (hardcover) -- ISBN 978-1-63470-071-9 (pdf) -- ISBN 978-1-63470-044-3 (paperback) --
ISBN 978-1-63470-098-6 (ebook)
  1. Downhill skiing--Juvenile literature. 2. Extreme sports--Juvenile literature. 3. ESPN X-Games--Juvenile literature.
I. Title.

  GV854.315.L65 2015
  796.93'5--dc23

                2015006303

ABOUT THE AUTHOR

Dr. Virginia Loh-Hagan is an author, university professor, former classroom teacher, and curriculum designer. She skied one bunny slope and called it a day. She hung out in the ski lodge instead. She lives in San Diego with her very tall husband and very naughty dogs. To learn more about her, visit www.virginialoh.com.

Table of Contents

Nothing is Impossible!

Who is Candide Thovex? Who is Cody Townsend? What is the Grand Teton? Who is Bill Briggs? What is extreme snow skiing?

Candide Thovex zooms down the mountain. He jumps off cliffs. He does backflips and turns. He avoids hitting skiers. He jumps over them. He weaves through trees. He zips through dark tunnels. He skis through a restaurant. He skis on the railing. He skis onto a ski lift. These are all fun stunts for him.

Cody Townsend peers down "The Crack." It's in Alaska. It's only 5 to 6 feet (1.5 to 1.8 meters) wide. It's a straight mountain wall. He skis down at high speed. He weaves around sharp rocks. He said, "That's the scariest thing I've ever done."

Both men know how to **shred**. They ski hard and fast.

The Grand Teton is in Wyoming. It's 13,770 feet (4,197 m) high. It's mainly cliffs. It's steep. There are strong winds. Falling means dying. Skiing this mountain was thought to be impossible.

Extreme skiers ride insane, or crazy, ski lines.

Bill Briggs did it. He was born without a hip joint. He had surgeries. Doctors told him he'd need a wheelchair. He said, "Anything you want to do, you can make a way of doing." He created his own gear.

Briggs was first to ski the Grand Teton. He did it in 1971. He couldn't ski some parts. So he used ropes to **descend**.

Nobody believed Bill Briggs skied the Grand Teton. A local newspaperwoman flew over the mountain to see his tracks.

Spotlight Biography: Andre and Suki Horton

Andre and Andreana "Suki" Horton are top-ranked skiers. Andre started at the age of 5. Suki started at age 3. They have won contests. They skied for the U.S. Ski Team. They are brother and sister. They're from Alaska. Their mother is white. Their father is African American. They opened the sport to young African American athletes. Suki said, "When I saw Tiger Woods, and the way that everyone started playing golf after he won, I thought, maybe I can make an impact by making the U.S. Ski Team. I realized that what I do out there could affect a lot of people." Andre was the first African American to win the International Ski Federation contest. He also was the first African American to be on the U.S. Ski Team. The National Brotherhood of Skiers supported them. It is a group dedicated to helping African American skiers.

Descend means to go down. He made first descents of other mountains. He skied in places where no one had

Extreme snow skiing is also called big mountain skiing or steep hill skiing.

skied before. He's the "father of extreme skiing." He led the way for Thovex and Townsend.

Extreme snow skiing is a type of free skiing. Skiers descend steep slopes. The slopes are at least 45 degrees.

Extreme skiers make the impossible possible. They ski fast. They ski fiercely. They ski away from **groomed** ski trails. Groomed means prepared. They prefer **backcountry** places. Backcountry means undeveloped. They jump **obstacles**. Obstacles are things like rocks, trees, and cliffs. They use obstacles to get air. Obstacles are fun. But they're also dangerous.

Anything covered with snow can be skied. Sometimes, there are things that can't be skied. So they jump. They land on things that can be skied. Nothing stops them!

"Extreme skiers make the impossible possible."

First Descents

What does a first descent mean? Why is 1971 an important year? Who is Sylvain Saudan? Who is Fritz Stammberger? Who is Yuichiro Miura?

Extreme skiers want to be the first to descend. They look for mountainous **terrain**, or land. They want to be the first to ski down it.

The year 1971 was important for extreme skiing. Sylvain Saudan had a first descent. He skied down Oregon's Mount Hood. It's 11,239 feet (3,425 m) high. He's had other first descents. He's the first to ski 26,000-foot (7,925 m) peaks. He is called "skier of the impossible."

Saudan invented the windshield wiper turn. It helps skiers ski steep slopes. Skiers make short jump turns. They control their speed.

Saudan's extreme. He survived a helicopter crash. He skied down Mount Fuji without snow. He said, "I don't live for the mountain. I couldn't live without her. I live with her."

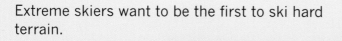

Extreme skiers want to be the first to ski hard terrain.

Fritz Stammberger descended Maroon Bells in 1971. It's in Colorado. It's known as "Deadly Bells." People have died on this mountain. It's steep. It has many cliffs. It has loose rocks. Stammberger camped on the mountain. He fell off a 15-foot (4.5 m) cliff. He didn't use ropes. He didn't have a support team. But he lived.

NAILED IT!

Advice From The Field: How to Fall

A ski instructor said, "If you aren't falling down a lot, you aren't trying hard enough." Extreme skiers have to be willing to fall and fail before winning big. When expert skiers fall, they tuck their thumbs into fists. Breaking thumbs is a common injury. This is called skier's thumb. Skiers will try to break falls with their hands. Expert skiers know how to fall correctly. They fall uphill. This means falling toward the mountain slope. They can stop faster. They don't have to twist as much. They also don't slide as much.

To be the first to do something is scary. Skiers don't know anything about the trail.

Around the same time, Yuichiro Miura skied down Mount Everest. This is the highest peak on Earth. He was the first to do this. He descended nearly 4,200 feet (1,280 m). He used a **parachute** to slow his descent. A parachute looks like a balloon top.

Miura descended the highest mountain in each of the seven continents. He escaped an **avalanche**. He's known as the "godfather of extreme skiing."

These skiers developed extreme skiing. Their descents opened doors for others.

Avalanche!

Why are avalanches dangerous to extreme skiers? What other dangers do extreme skiers face? Who are some extreme skiers who have lost their lives for the sport?

Trevor Petersen starred in many movies, films, and magazines. He was the first to descend many mountains in North America. He skied in Chamonix, France. The town is called the Death Sport Capital of the World. He died in an avalanche there.

Ronnie Berlack and Bryce Astle were on the U.S. Ski Team. They were in Austria. They were training. They left the groomed slopes. They set off an avalanche. They died.

Avalanches are very dangerous. It's when snow flows quickly down a slope. All skiers should carry **beacons**. They give off signals. Rescuers get the signals. They find people buried under snow. Avalanche dogs can also help rescue skiers. They can smell people under the snow.

Extreme snow skiers take risks. Avalanches are a real danger.

Extreme Snow Skiing: Know the Lingo

Big air: high, long jump

Daffy: legs spread apart like a running stride

Digger: falling or crashing

Gnarly: beyond rad, beyond extreme, perfection; dangerous

Hucking: dropping off a cliff

Kicker: jumps for doing tricks

Kosak: split in the air

Mandatory air: hucking a cliff that cannot be avoided

No-fall zone: terrain that is so dangerous that a fall would mean certain death

Powder: snow

Rad: cool, radical

Run: from top of the slope to bottom, includes obstacles and tricks

Skinning: special climbing skins that backcountry adventurers attach to the base of skis that allow them to grip while going up and glide while sliding

Sick: really awesome

Extreme skiers can get hurt descending a mountain.

Avalanches are not the only danger. Mountain weather is **unpredictable**. That means no one knows what's going to happen. Sunshine can turn into a storm. Extreme skiers face strong winds. They face below-freezing temperatures. It may be cold. But they can get badly sunburned. The sun reflects off snow.

Extreme skiers must be aware of all types of danger. Sudden dips could trip skiers. Obstacles under snow could hurt them. They need to be careful of unknown terrain. Falling could mean hitting rocks on the way down. Mistakes lead to injury or death. Skiers lose teeth. They break bones. They ruin their knees and spines.

Doug Coombs was a great skier. He was skiing with friends. One friend fell. He tried to rescue him. Then Coombs fell. He had fallen about 1,500 feet (457 m). He died.

Sarah Burke won many medals. She was the first woman to land a 1080. It's two backflips with three full turns. She died in a training accident. She was skiing on the **halfpipe**. A halfpipe is a U-shaped ramp. She fell on her head. She had a heart attack. She died from her injuries.

Shane McConkey was doing a trick he'd done before. He was on a 2,000-foot (609.6 m) cliff. He jumped with a parachute. He did a double backflip. He couldn't release his skis. His skis tangled up in his parachute. He died.

It's sad when young skiers die. Many skiers are friends. Losing friends is hard.

Extreme skiers risk their lives. They practice and prepare.

Types of Snow Skiers

What is freestyle snow skiing? What is a hotdogger? What is big air skiing? What is off-piste skiing? What is heliskiing?

Extreme skiers love the risk, speed, and thrill. They do amazing things with skis. There are few rules. There's lots of danger.

Freestyle skiers do tricks. They do **aerial** stunts. Aerials are tricks in the air. They do long jumps. They do high-**altitude** drops. This means they fall from very high places. They do spins, flips, and grabs. They do whatever they can. They go as fast as they can.

Hotdoggers are skiers who show off. They do hard and dangerous moves. They launch tricks off jumps. They ski over bumps. They add aerials to their runs. These include spins, flips, twists, and **spreads**. Spreads are doing the splits in the air.

Big air skiers do grabs, flips, and spins in midair. Vincent Gagnier crashed on a rail. He broke his back. He recovered.

Freestyle skiers have the freedom to do tricks and stunts.

He won a gold medal in a big air contest. He said, "I did two tricks that I never tried before, and they both worked out." He's known for his style.

Off-piste skiing is very popular. Off-piste means skiing down ungroomed trails or in the backcountry.

NAILED IT!

That Happened?!?

Peter Olenick is a Norwegian daredevil. He skied down a 200-foot-long (61 m) escalator. It's the longest escalator in Great Britain. An escalator is a moving staircase. It was at the Angel Tube station in London. He had a camera strapped to his helmet and filmed the stunt. The station was upset with him. An official said, "This is a dangerous, stupid, and irresponsible act that could have resulted in serious injury or death to not only the individual concerned but also other passengers." Olenick has been described as the "Norwegian nutter." Nutter means a crazy person.

Vincent Gagnier competed in the X Games. They are a contest for extreme sports.

Helicopters drop off skiers at the top of mountains.

Some extreme skiers take helicopters to ski off-piste. This is called heliskiing. They ski down. Then helicopters take skiers to the top. They can ski many times. That saves time and energy. Helicopters allow skiers to ski anywhere. They can go to faraway places.

Hans Gmoser developed heliskiing. He said, "A person should have wings to carry them where their dreams go. But sometimes a pair of skis makes a good substitute." He was dedicated to taking skiers to their slopes.

"A person should have wings to carry them where their dreams go."

New Ways to Be Extreme!

What are variations of extreme snow skiing? What is ski-BASE jumping? What is ski gliding? What is snow kiting?

Extreme skiers look for new opportunities. They combine sports. They create new ones.

Some slopes end with huge cliffs. Skiers jump off these cliffs. They'll open a **canopy**. A canopy is a special parachute. This is extreme ski-BASE jumping.

Ski-BASE jumping combines BASE jumping and skiing. BASE jumpers jump from objects. They jump from buildings, **antennas**, **spans**, and earth. Ski-BASE jumpers ski off roofs, towers, bridges, and cliffs. They ski at high speeds. They release their skis. They open a canopy.

Ski gliding is also called ski flying. Skiers ski off a cliff. They're strapped to a **hang glider.** A hang glider is a flying device. They look like wings. Skiers fly for a while.

Snow kites help skiers get air and speed. Skiers are strapped to a large kite. They descend. The kite pulls skiers across or above the terrain. They can avoid dangerous objects.

Some skiers combine BASE jumping and skiing. They BASE jump from mountains wearing their skis. They open parachutes.

When Extreme Is Too Extreme!

Miles Daisher is a member of the Red Bull Air Force team. This is a stunt he loves. He skis off a cliff. He's strapped to a paraglider. A paraglider is a parachute wing. He has a canopy. He's going really fast. He catches air. He lets go of his skis in midair. He lets go of the paraglider. He free-falls for a bit. Free fall means he's flying in the air. Then he opens his canopy. There isn't a name for this stunt. It's known as a "Speed-Ride-Ski-Drop-Sky-Dive." Daisher said, "It's so much fun, and it's the way of the future. You come to a cliff that's too big to jump off with skis, and you just fly right off it."

They can just fly over them. Snow kiting combines kite surfing and skiing.

There's no end to what extreme skiers can create. They make things up as they go!

Variations of extreme skiing all involve steep slopes.

Did You Know?

- Skier Bill Briggs can play the banjo. He also yodels really well. He played music with the famous singer Bob Dylan. It was at a wedding in Jackson Hole, Wyoming.

- The World Extreme Skiing Championships were held from 1991 to 2000. This led to the growth of the sport. It also inspired the idea for the X Games.

- Sometimes, ski resorts set off avalanches with explosives. They do this to stop unexpected snow slides.

- Norway had a civil war in 1206. Two Vikings put on skis. They rescued a baby prince from invaders. They skied 35 miles (56 kilometers) without poles. They might have been the world's first extreme skiers.

- In the 1970s, French skiers came up with the term extreme skiing. The original motto of extreme skiing was, "If you fall, you die."

- Fritz Stammberger set a record. He had the highest ski descent. He skied from 24,000 feet (7,315 m) in Tibet. It's a country in Asia. He also skied and climbed in the Himalayas. In 1975, he went missing. His wife believes he was in the CIA and was killed because he was a spy.

Consider This!

TAKE A POSITION! Some skiers prefer skiing at resorts. They don't see the need to ski in the backcountry or off-piste. They think it's too dangerous. They don't think it's worth the risks. What do you think? Argue your point with reasons and evidence.

SAY WHAT? Reread chapter 5. Extreme sports combine to form new sports. Learn about extreme BASE jumping and kite surfing. Explain how extreme skiing is similar to and different from these sports.

THINK ABOUT IT! The National Brotherhood of Skiers promotes African American skiers. There aren't many African American skiers. The organization lists three factors: geography, history, and money. African Americans don't tend to live near ski resorts. They don't come from families that ski. So skiing is not passed down from one generation to another. And skiing costs a lot of money. It's hard for racers to get sponsorships. What do you think about this? How should more people of color be encouraged to participate in skiing?

SEE A DIFFERENT SIDE! Sarah Burke donated her organs. Organ donations save lives. Some people disagree with organ donation. Learn more about the different perspectives. What do you think about organ donation?

Learn More: Resources

Primary Sources

The Edge of Never: A True Story of Skiing's Big-Mountain Tribe, a documentary about extreme skiing and the relationship between Trevor and Kye Petersen (directed by William A. Kerig, 2009), www.edgeofneverfilm.com

Steep, a documentary about extreme skiing (written and directed by Mark Obenhaus, 2007).

Secondary Sources

Catel, Patrick. *Skiing.* Chicago: Raintree, 2013.

Gifford, Clive. *Skiing.* New York: PowerKids Press, 2011.

Maurer, Tracy Nelson. *Snow Skiing.* Vero Beach, FL: Rourke Publishing, 2002.

Web Sites

National Ski and Board Safety Association: http://safe2skiandboard.org

United States of America Snowboard and Freeski Association: https://www.usasa.org

X Games—Skiing: http://xgames.espn.go.com/skiing/

Glossary

aerial (AIR-ee-uhl) happening in the air

altitude (AL-ti-tood) the height of something above sea level

antennas (an-TEN-uhz) towers used to broadcast TV, radio, cell phone, or other signals

avalanche (AV-uh-lanch) when snow flows quickly down a slope

backcountry (BAK-kun-tree) natural or undeveloped places

beacons (BEE-kuhnz) devices that signal location

canopy (KAN-uh-pee) a special parachute for BASE jumpers that looks like a bird's wing

descend (dih-SEND) to go down

groomed (GROOMD) ski trails that are prepared and established

halfpipe (HAF-pipe) a U-shaped ramp

hang glider (HANG GLY-dur) a flying device that looks like wings

obstacles (AHB-stuh-kuhlz) things like rocks, trees, cliffs, or ramps

off-piste (AWF PEAST) skiing on ungroomed trails or in the backcountry

parachute (PA-ruh-shoot) a piece of strong, light fabric attached to thin ropes that helps skydivers slow down their fall through the air

shred (SHRED) skiing hard and fast

spans (SPANZ) man-made or natural bridges or arches that cover an opening

spreads (SPREDZ) tricks that look like doing the splits in the air

terrain (tuh-RAYN) land

unpredictable (un-pree-DIK-tuh-buhl) not able to know what's going to happen

Index